STEP·B

MEXICAN
Cooking

Your Promise of Success

Welcome to the world of Confident Cooking, created for you
in our test kitchen, where recipes are double-tested by our team
of home economists to achieve a high standard of success.

MURDOCH BOOKS®
New York • Sydney • London • Vancouver

BASIC MEXICAN PANTRY

*Most ingredients for Mexican cooking are familiar and readily available.
The exception, Masa Harina, can be found at large supermarkets or
Mexican food stores.*

Avocado: Pear-shaped fruit with a dark green or purple skin. The flesh has a slightly nutty flavor and has a creamy yellow–green color. It is usually eaten raw in salads or mashed and made into a dip. Mexicans generally use the purple-skinned avocadoes, which are creamier and have more flavor.

Bell Peppers: These are used extensively in Mexican cooking. Choose from green, red, yellow or orange peppers. They have a mild sweet flavor. Bell peppers are charred under the broiler to give them a smokey roasted flavor. Cover with a towel until cool and remove the blackened skin.

Chilies: Available fresh, dried, or powdered. Chilies are used extensively in Mexican cooking. Adjust the amount to suit your taste. Fresh chili peppers are generally hotter than dried.

Jalapeno Chili Peppers: Ranging from hot to very hot in flavor, jalapenos are dark green, short and stumpy. Look for them in your grocer's produce section or in jars with other condiments or Mexican foods. You can substitute any type of fresh hot chili pepper for a jalepeno.

Cilantro: Also known as fresh coriander or Chinese parsley, it has a pungent, almost musty odor and taste that is used extensively in Mexican cooking. Look for bundles of fresh cilantro in the produce section near the fresh parsley or herbs.

Cinnamon: A favorite flavoring in Mexico and used in both sweet and savory dishes. Available ground or in sticks.

Cloves: An aromatic flavoring in sweet and savory dishes. Available in bud or ground form.

Corn: Mexicans use both fresh and dried corn, often referred to as Masa Harina. Buy fresh ears of corn during the summer months or all year long in the frozen or canned form. Fresh corn is best when cooked just after it is picked. When buying fresh corn, look for bright, healthy-looking green husks. Pull the husks back and look

or plump, juicy kernels. Avoid buying fresh corn wrapped in plastic wrap.

Cumin: Used in seed or powdered form, it has a somewhat bitter, pungent flavor.

Flat Plate: A thin earthenware plate used for cooking tortillas. A heavy skillet may be substituted.

Huevos: Another name for eggs. Huevos Rancheros means 'ranch' or 'country-style' eggs.

Lard: Pork fat. Lard is commonly used in Mexican cooking, but the recipes in this book use olive oil as a healthier alternative. If you prefer the flavor of lard, substitute equal amounts of lard for the oil in the recipes.

Masa Harina: Finely ground corn used for making tortillas and other baked products.

Pale yellow in color, it can be purchased in grocery stores or at Mexican food stores or specialty shops.

Onions: Mexicans prefer white onions for their sharper flavor, but the milder Spanish or red onions are sometimes used as well.

Pepitas: Pumpkin seeds with the skin removed. Green in color, they can be bought from supermarkets or health food stores. They are sold raw or roasted.

Refried Beans: Pinto beans fried to an almost paste-like consistency. Look for them in cans at the

grocery store. You can make your own by frying canned and drained pinto beans in oil or lard and then mashing them with a potato masher. For a healthier option, look for cans of no-fat refried beans.

Snapper: This fish is a favorite in Mexican cookery. Reddish in color with a distinctive bump on its head. Look for firm flesh and bright bulging eyes.

Tacos: Tortillas which have been folded and fried until crisp. Ready-made taco shells are sold in supermarkets.

Tortillas: Very popular thin flat breads made from Masa Harina in a variety of sizes. Corn and flour tortillas are used interchangeably.

3

Cut avocado in half and remove seed with the blade of a sharp knife.

Peel avocado and mash flesh in a bowl using a fork.

STARTERS AND SOUPS

Nearly all Mexican food has a 'bite' to it, owing to the liberal use of chili peppers. These starters and soups are designed to make your taste buds tingle.

Guacamole

A favorite dip.

Preparation time:
20 minutes
Cooking time:
None
Serves 6

2 ripe avocadoes	⅓ cup sour cream
1 small onion	1 tablespoon lemon
1 medium tomato	juice
1 tablespoon chopped	Tabasco sauce, to taste
cilantro	

1 Cut avocadoes in half and remove the seed with the blade of a sharp knife.
2 Peel avocadoes and place flesh in medium bowl. Mash well with a fork until smooth.
3 Finely chop the onion and tomato and mix with chopped cilantro.
4 Add to avocado in bowl with remaining ingredients and mix well. Serve as a dip with tortilla chips or as one of the filling mixtures for tacos.
Note: Avocado flesh turns brown when exposed to air. To help prevent this, bury an avocado seed in the dip and cover with plastic wrap.

HINT
To remove seed without damaging avocado flesh, insert the blade of a sharp knife into the seed. Pull the knife away and the seed will come with it.
Guacamole Melt makes a delicious snack or breakfast dish. Pile Guacamole onto toast, sprinkle with shredded cheese and crumbled cooked bacon and broil until the cheese melts.

Finely chop onion, tomato and cilantro. Squeeze 1 tablespoon lemon juice.

Mix together all ingredients in a bowl and serve as a dip with tortilla chips.

Toasted Pepita Dip with Tortilla Chips

Preparation time:
  10 minutes
Cooking time:
  20 minutes
Serves 4–6

TORTILLA CHIPS
8 6-inch corn tortillas
vegetable oil
salt

TOASTED PEPITA DIP
1 cup shelled pumpkin seeds (pepitas)
1 clove garlic

1 medium onion, coarsely chopped
1 tablespoon lemon juice
⅓ cup olive oil

---

1 To make Tortilla Chips: Cut each corn tortilla into 4 wedges. Heat about 1 inch of oil in a large skillet. Fry tortilla wedges, a few at a time, in hot oil until golden brown, turning to brown evenly. Drain on paper towels. Salt lightly and let cool.

2 To make Pepita Dip: Place pumpkin seeds on a baking sheet. Broil for 2 minutes or until the seeds swell and pop; remove and cool.

3 Place pumpkin seeds, garlic, onion, lemon juice and oil in a food processor bowl. Process 30 seconds or until smooth. Serve with tortilla chips.

Note: Pepitas are shelled pumpkin seeds. They are available in supermarkets and health food stores and typically labeled 'pumpkin seeds'. The seeds are green. Do not confuse them with white-colored salted pumpkin seeds which have to be shelled before eaten. You can store the dip in a covered container in the refrigerator for up to 1 week. It is equally good served with vegetable sticks.

Cut each corn tortilla into 4 wedges, making a total of 32 wedges.

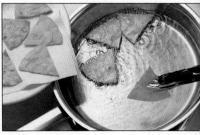

Fry tortilla wedges in hot oil until golden brown; turn to brown evenly.

Place all ingredients for Pepita Dip into food processor bowl.

Process Pepita Dip until smooth. Serve with tortilla chips.

Tortillas

Mexican bread, tortillas are served with most meals.

> 1¼ cups all-purpose flour
> 1¼ cups Masa Harina tortilla flour
> 1½ cups warm water

1 Combine all-purpose flour and tortilla flour in a large mixing bowl. Make a well in the center. Gradually add warm water. Stir until a firm dough forms. Turn out onto a lightly floured surface. Knead for 3 minutes or until smooth.

2 Divide dough into

Preparation time:
1 hour
Cooking time:
20 minutes
Makes 16 8-inch
or 20 6-inch or
40 4-inch tortillas

desired portions. Roll out one portion at a time on a lightly floured surface until very thin (about paper thickness). Set aside and repeat with remaining portions. Keep the unrolled portions wrapped in plastic wrap to prevent them from drying out.

3 Heat an ungreased skillet over medium-hot heat. Place one tortilla in dry pan. When edges begin to curl slightly, turn and

cook other side.
1–2 minutes on each side is ample cooking time. If residual flour begins to burn in pan, wipe out with a paper towel.

Note: Tortillas will soften on standing. Tear into pieces and serve with dips or roll up with filling for a burrito. Tortillas will keep fresh for 1 week in an airtight container. Warm them briefly in the oven or microwave oven. Stale tortillas can be torn into bite-size pieces and fried in hot oil to make tortilla chips. Use them as a snack or serve them with salsa or a dip.

Combine flours in a bowl. Make a well in center and add water.

Knead dough on a lightly floured surface for 3 minutes or until smooth.

Divide dough into portions and roll out into very thin circles.

Cook tortillas, one at a time, in a hot skillet, turning when edges begin to curl.

Huevos Rancheros

Preparation time:
1 hour
Cooking time:
35 minutes
Serves 6

---

2 small red bell peppers, halved and seeded	1 medium green bell pepper, finely chopped
1 tablespoon olive oil	3 tablespoons tomato paste
1 tablespoon olive oil, extra	2 jalapeno chili peppers, finely sliced
1 teaspoon ground oregano	6 6-inch tortillas
1 small onion, finely chopped	6 eggs, fried or poached
	⅔ cup shredded cheese

---

1 Brush red peppers with oil. Broil about 10 minutes or until skin turns black. Cover with a damp towel until cool. Peel off skin. Place bell pepper flesh in a food processor bowl. Process 30 seconds or until smooth. Set aside.

2 Heat extra oil in a medium saucepan. Add oregano, onion, green pepper and tomato paste. Cook until onion is tender. Stir in red pepper purée and jalapenos. Heat gently.

3 To serve, place one fried or poached egg on a tortilla. Top with some of the red pepper sauce and sprinkle with cheese. **Note:** Mexicans eat Huevos Rancheros for breakfast or lunch. Usually served hot, it may also be eaten cold. The red pepper sauce can be used as a dip with tortilla chips. Or, serve it as a fiery addition to scrambled eggs or meat dishes. Store the sauce in a covered container in the refrigerator for up to 5 days.

Cover blacked red bell peppers with a damp towel until cool.

Peel off black skin from peppers and purée the flesh in a food processor.

Stir red pepper purée and sliced jalapenos into sauce; heat gently for 1 minute.

Place cooked egg on a tortilla, top with red pepper sauce and sprinkle with cheese.

Chicken and Pea Soup

Preparation time:
20 minutes
Cooking time:
40 minutes
Serves 6–8

---

1 cup yellow split peas
⅔ cup green split peas
1 small onion,
chopped
2 bay leaves
10 peppercorns
5 cups water

1½ pounds boneless
skinless chicken
breasts
3 cups chicken stock
1 tablespoon chopped
cilantro

---

1 Combine split peas, onion, bay leaves, peppercorns and water in a large pan. Bring to a boil; reduce heat. Simmer, covered, about 30 minutes or until peas are tender, stirring occasionally. Skim the top while simmering to remove froth. Remove from heat; cool. Remove and discard bay leaves.

2 Trim chicken of excess fat. Heat chicken stock in a skillet. Add chicken. Cover and simmer about 10 minutes or until tender and no longer pink. Drain; strain and reserve stock. Cool chicken and cut into strips. Set aside.

3 Pour split pea mixture into a food processor bowl. Process 1–2 minutes or until smooth. Return mixture to saucepan. Add cooked chicken and reserved stock. Stir in cilantro and heat through.

Note: This soup can be made several hours in advance. Reheat gently just before serving. Lentils can be used instead of split peas. They cook faster, so reduce the cooking time slightly.

HINT
Split peas will cook faster if you soak them overnight in cold water. Do not add salt. Drain and add fresh water before cooking.

Combine split peas, onion, bay leaves, peppercorns and water in a saucepan.

Skim the top of the soup while it simmers to remove surface froth.

Poach chicken in chicken stock until tender. Cut into strips when cool.

Purée split pea mixture and add chicken, stock and chopped cilantro.

Creamy Corn and Tomato Soup

Preparation time:
  35 minutes
Cooking time:
  15 minutes
Serves 4–6

---

2 teaspoons olive oil
1 medium onion,
  finely chopped
1 teaspoon chicken
  bouillon granules
3 medium tomatoes
1 15-ounce can tomato
  purée

1 8 ¾-ounce can
  creamed corn
1 7-ounce can whole
  kernel corn,
  drained
chili powder, to taste
sour cream and
  tortillas, to serve

---

1 Heat oil in a large saucepan. Add onion and granules and cook until onion is tender.
2 Peel tomatoes, cut in half and remove seeds with a spoon; chop flesh. Add to onion mixture. Stir in purée, creamed corn and whole kernel corn. Season with chili powder. Heat through. Dollop sour cream on each serving and serve with tortillas.

Note: This soup can be frozen in an airtight container for up to 4 weeks. Make this quick soup anytime by keeping the ingredients in your cupboard or pantry.

Heat oil and cook onion and chicken bouillon granules until onion is tender.

Peel tomatoes, cut in half and remove the seeds with a small spoon.

Add chopped tomatoes to onions in pan. Stir in tomato purée and creamed corn.

Add whole kernel corn and chili powder to saucepan. Heat through.

Trim lamb of excess fat; roll up and tie it securely with string.

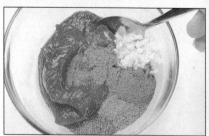

Stir together tomato paste, chili powder, pepper, garlic, cumin and cinnamon.

LAMB, BEEF & PORK

Mexican meat dishes are spicy and tasty, with the warm flavors of cinnamon and cumin predominating.

Roasted Lamb with Chili Powder

Preparation time:
   10 minutes
Cooking time:
   35 minutes
Serves 4

---

1 pound loin of lamb
   or pork tenderloin
1/3 cup tomato paste
1/2 teaspoon chili
   powder
1/4 teaspoon ground
   pepper
2 cloves garlic, crushed

1 teaspoon ground
   cumin
1/2 teaspoon ground
   cinnamon
1/4 cup shredded
   cheddar cheese

---

1 Preheat oven to 350°F. Trim meat of excess fat. Roll the meat and tie it securely with string.
2 Combine tomato paste, chili powder, pepper, garlic, cumin and cinnamon in a small bowl. Spread this mixture all over the meat. Sprinkle with cheese.
5 Place in a shallow baking dish and roast lamb for 35 minutes or until medium (150°–155°F). (Pork should be 160°F.) Cover with foil and let stand 5 minutes before slicing. Serve with roasted vegetables and warm corn tortillas.
Note: Lamb cooked with spices in this way is also excellent served cold for sandwiches.

> **HINT**
> Keep a special board for chopping onion, garlic and chili peppers.

Spread the chili powder mixture all over the meat with a spatula or knife.

Place lamb in a shallow baking dish and sprinkle with shredded cheese.

Lamb Empanados

Mexico's meat pie.

Preparation time:
1 hour
Cooking time:
20 minutes
Serves 6

---

8 ounces ground lamb
½ small onion, finely chopped
½ medium green bell pepper, finely chopped
1 small carrot, finely chopped
2 tablespoons tomato paste
1 teaspoon ground cinnamon
2 teaspoons brown sugar

PASTRY
2 cups all-purpose flour
¼ teaspoon salt
½ cup cold butter, cut up
½ cup cold milk
2 tablespoons butter, softened
1 beaten egg

---

1 In a medium skillet cook lamb and onion over medium heat until meat is brown. Drain. Add bell pepper, carrot, tomato paste, cinnamon and sugar. Mix well. Remove from heat; cool.

2 Preheat oven to 400°F. Lightly grease a baking sheet. Set aside.

3 To make Pastry: Place flour and salt in a food processor bowl. Process until combined. Add butter and process mixture until it resembles fine bread crumbs. Add cold milk and process to make a soft dough. Turn dough out onto a lightly floured surface. Knead gently. Divide dough into three equal portions.

4 On a lightly floured surface, roll each portion into an 8-inch square. Spread two of the squares with softened butter. Stack all three dough squares on top of each other, with the unbuttered square on top. Roll out the layers together.

5 To assemble: Cut out six 6-inch circles from pastry. Divide meat mixture evenly between the circles. Brush edges with egg. Fold in half, pressing edges together with the tines of a fork. Place on prepared baking sheet. Brush pastry with remaining egg. Bake for 15–20 minutes or until puffed and golden. Serve with a green salad.

Note: Freeze unbaked empanados in an airtight plastic bag for 4 weeks. To bake, place frozen pastries on baking sheet and bake in a 400°F oven for 25–30 minutes or until golden brown and heated through. Try making them with taco filling.

Add bell pepper, carrot, tomato paste, cinnamon and sugar to cooked lamb.

Divide dough into 3 equal portions and roll each portion into a square.

Spread two dough squares with butter and stack squares on top of each other.

Place spoonfuls of filling on each dough circle, brush edge with egg and fold.

Tex Mex Chili con Carne

Preparation time:
30 minutes
Cooking time:
50 minutes
Serves 4

1 tablespoon olive oil
2 cloves garlic, crushed
1½ pounds top round
   steak, cut into
   ¾-inch cubes
1 large onion, chopped
2 bay leaves
1 cup tomato juice
1 16-ounce can whole
   tomatoes, crushed

1 16-ounce can red
   kidney beans,
   drained
1–2 tablespoons chili
   powder
1 teaspoon ground
   cumin
½ teaspoon ground
   oregano
¼ teaspoon cayenne
   pepper

1 Heat oil and garlic in a large pan. Cook meat in batches over medium heat until well browned.

2 Stir in onion, bay leaves, tomato juice and tomatoes. Bring to a boil; reduce heat.

3 Cover and simmer for 40 minutes or until meat is very tender and liquid has reduced by half. Stir in beans and spices. Cook for 10 minutes more. Serve with Guacamole and corn chips.

Cook cubed meat in batches in hot oil and garlic until well browned.

Add onion, bay leaves, tomato juice and tomatoes to meat in saucepan.

When meat is very tender and liquid has reduced, stir in kidney beans.

Spice up the chili with chili powder, cumin, oregano and cayenne pepper.

Spicy Beef and Bean Tacos

Preparation time:
25 minutes
Cooking time:
15 minutes
Serves 4

---

8 ounces ground beef	*12 taco shells*
1 small onion, finely chopped	*1/2 cup shredded cheddar cheese*
1/3 cup tomato paste	*2 small carrots, grated*
1 teaspoon chili powder	*2 medium tomatoes, sliced*
1 teaspoon ground cumin	*1/2 small lettuce, shredded*
1 teaspoon ground coriander	
1 16-ounce can refried beans	

1 In a medium skillet cook ground beef and onion until meat is brown and onion is tender. Drain off fat.
2 Add tomato paste, chili powder, cumin, coriander and refried beans. Mix well. Cook, stirring occasionally, for 2–3 minutes or until mixture is hot.
3 To serve, preheat oven to 350°F. Place taco shells over the rungs of the oven rack. (This will prevent them from closing up while they heat.) Heat for about 8 minutes until they are crisp. Alternatively, taco shells can be heated in a microwave oven. Follow the package instructions. Fill shells with beef mixture, cheese, carrots, tomatoes and lettuce. Sour cream or Guacamole can also be added, if desired.

Note: Beef mixture can be cooked and frozen for 4 weeks in an airtight container. Thaw meat mixture and reheat in a saucepan over low heat. Taco shells also freeze well. They do not have to be thawed before reheating.

Cook ground beef and chopped onion until meat is brown and onion is tender.

Add tomato paste, chili powder, cumin and coriander to meat mixture and stir well.

Stir in refried beans and cook for 2–3 minutes or until mixture is hot.

Place meat mixture in taco shells and top with cheese, carrots, tomato and lettuce.

Burritos

Serve hot or cold.

Preparation time:
15 minutes
Cooking time:
40 minutes
Serves 4

1 pound boneless top round roast or boneless shoulder pot roast	*1 medium onion, finely sliced*
	4 cloves
	1 bay leaf
1 tablespoon olive oil	*2½ cups beef stock*
1 cinnamon stick	*8 8-inch flour tortillas*

1 Trim meat of excess fat; cut into 1-inch cubes. Heat oil in a large saucepan, add onion. Cook until golden brown.

2 Add meat, cinnamon stick, cloves, bay leaf and beef stock. Bring to a boil; reduce heat. Simmer, uncovered, for 40 minutes or until meat is tender and liquid is almost all absorbed. Remove and discard the cinnamon stick, cloves and bay leaf.

3 Shred meat with two forks. Roll meat up in tortillas. Serve with Tomato Salsa and salad.

Note: The meat mixture will keep, covered, in the refrigerator for up to 3 days.

Trim meat of excess fat. Cut into 1-inch cubes.

Cook sliced onion in oil over medium heat until golden brown.

Add meat to pan with cinnamon stick, cloves, bay leaf and beef stock.

When meat is cooked and liquid almost absorbed, shred meat with two forks.

Pork Ribs with Tomato and Pineapple

Preparation time:
30 minutes
Cooking time:
30 minutes
Serves 4

---

2 teaspoons coriander
seeds, crushed (see
Note)
1 teaspoon cumin
seeds, crushed
1/2 cup all-purpose
flour
2 pounds pork spare
ribs, cut into
1 1/2-inch pieces
1 tablespoon olive oil

1 medium onion,
chopped
2 16-ounce cans whole
tomatoes, crushed
1 tablespoon tomato
paste
2 medium zucchini,
sliced
1 cup fresh pineapple
wedges

---

1 Combine crushed coriander seeds, cumin seeds and flour in a medium bowl. Dust pork ribs with this spiced flour mixture; shake off excess. Reserve 1 tablespoon of spiced flour mixture. Sift remaining spiced flour mixture, discard flour and add spices to reserved spiced flour mixture.

2 Heat oil in a large skillet. Cook meat in batches over medium-high heat until well browned. Drain on paper towels. Add onion and cook until tender. Add reserved spiced flour mixture; stir over low heat.

3 Add tomatoes and tomato paste; stir to combine. Bring to a boil and allow to thicken, stirring constantly. Return pork to pan. Cover and simmer until pork is tender. Add zucchini and pineapple. Cook 10 minutes more.

Note: Crushing your own seeds releases a fresher, more pungent flavor. Use a mortar and pestle or coffee grinder. If not available, substitute ready-ground spices.

Crush coriander seeds and cumin seeds in a mortar and pestle.

Dust pork ribs in spiced flour and cook in batches in oil until well browned.

Add tomatoes and tomato paste to cooked onion in pan.

Add zucchini and pineapple to cooked rib mixture and cook 10 minutes more.

Mix together tomato, onion, tomato paste, cumin, coriander and Tabasco sauce.

Brush fish with a mixture of pepper, lemon juice and melted butter.

SEAFOOD

Mexicans love seafood and these tasty fish and shellfish dishes are fresh, simple to prepare and very quick.

Fish with Tomato Cheese Crust

Preparation time:
40 minutes
Cooking time:
15 minutes
Serves 4

2 medium ripe tomatoes, peeled, seeded, chopped	*¼ teaspoon ground pepper*
1 small onion, finely chopped	*1 tablespoon lemon juice*
2 tablespoons tomato paste	*2 tablespoons butter, melted*
½ teaspoon ground cumin	*4 medium whitefish fillets*
½ teaspoon ground coriander	*1 cup shredded cheddar cheese*
Tabasco, to taste	*⅔ cup fresh bread crumbs*

1 Preheat oven to 350°F. Brush a 15 x 10 x 1-inch baking pan with melted butter or oil. Place chopped tomato in a small bowl. Add onion, tomato paste, cumin, coriander and Tabasco sauce. Mix well; set aside.

2 Combine pepper, lemon juice and butter in a separate small bowl. Place fish fillets on prepared pan. Brush each fillet with pepper mixture and top with tomato mixture.

3 Sprinkle with combined cheese and bread crumbs. Bake for 15 minutes or until tender and fish flakes when tested with a fork. Serve with a green salad and warm tortillas.

Top fish with tomato mixture and sprinkle with cheese and bread crumb mixture.

To test fish, insert a fork into thickest part. If it flakes easily, then it is done.

Baked Fish with Bacon and Capers

Preparation time:
  25 minutes
Cooking time:
  40 minutes
Serves 2

2 small whole flounder, trout or catfish (about 10 ounces each)	*2 slices bacon, finely chopped*
lemon juice, to taste	*3 tablespoons white wine*
ground pepper, to taste	*1 tablespoon capers*
1 teaspoon olive oil	*2 tablespoons sour cream*
1 small onion, sliced	*⅓ cup light cream*

1 Preheat oven to 350°F. Scale fish, if necessary. Rinse fish; pat dry with paper towels. Place fish side-by-side in an ovenproof baking dish. Sprinkle fish with lemon juice and pepper; set aside.

2 Heat oil in a small saucepan. Add onion and bacon. Cook until onion is tender. Stir in wine, capers, sour cream and cream. Pour over fish. Bake 40 minutes or till fish flake easily with a fork. Serve with vegetables or a green salad.

Note: Use any small whole fish.

Place fish in an ovenproof dish; sprinkle with lemon juice and pepper.

Cook onion and bacon in oil until the onion is tender.

Stir in wine, capers, sour cream and cream. Mix well.

Pour the sauce over fish and bake for 40 minutes or until fish flakes with a fork.

Shrimp in Cilantro

Preparation time:
  25 minutes
Cooking time:
  10 minutes
Serves 4–6

24 green large shrimp	*1/3 cup chopped*
3 tablespoons butter	*cilantro*
1 clove garlic,	*2 teaspoons chopped*
crushed	*fresh chives*
1 tablespoon brown	*1 tablespoon sour*
sugar	*cream*
1/4 cup lime juice	

1 Shell shrimp, leaving tails intact; devein. Set aside.
2 Heat butter in a medium saucepan; add garlic, sugar, lime juice, cilantro, chives and sour cream. Mix well. Add shrimp. Cook and stir just until shrimp turn pink. Serve warm or cold.

Note: Oysters and scallops may also be cooked in the same way.

Cilantro, also called fresh coriander or Chinese parsley, is a pungent herb often used in Mexican cooking. Look for it in the produce section near fresh parsley and herbs.

Shell shrimp, leaving their tails intact. Remove veins.

Heat butter in pan, add garlic, sugar, lime juice, cilantro, chives and sour cream.

Once the cilantro mixture is hot and well combined, add the shrimp.

Cook the shrimp, stirring constantly, just until they turn pink. Do not overcook.

Spicy Seafood and Rice

Preparation time:
  45 minutes
Cooking time:
  20 minutes
Serves 4–6

---

2 cups vegetable or
  fish stock
10 mussels, scrubbed
2 medium calamari,
  sliced
10 medium shrimp,
  shelled and deveined
1 tablespoon olive oil
1/2 teaspoon ground
  cinnamon

1/2 teaspoon ground
  cloves
1 medium onion,
  finely chopped
1/3 cup tomato paste
1 1/2 cups long grain
  rice
1 1/2 cups water
1 10-ounce can baby
  clams, drained
lime juice, to taste

---

1 Place stock in a medium saucepan. Bring to a boil; reduce heat. Add mussels, calamari and shrimp. Simmer until mussel shells have opened and calamari and shrimp are just tender.

Remove with a slotted spoon; set aside and reserve stock. Discard any mussels that haven't opened.

2 Heat oil in a large saucepan. Add cinnamon, cloves, onion and tomato paste; stir over medium heat. Add rice, reduce heat to low. Stir rice 2 minutes or until lightly golden.

3 Combine reserved stock and water. Add one-quarter of stock mixture to the pan. Stir continuously for 4–5 minutes or until liquid is absorbed.

4 Repeat this process 3 times, stirring continuously, until all the liquid has been added and the rice is almost tender.

5 Add cooked seafood and clams. Stir in a little lime juice. Cover and let stand for 4 minutes. Serve immediately with Tomato Salsa and warm tortillas.

Mussels are cooked when their shells have opened. Discard unopened mussels.

Add cinnamon, cloves, onion, tomato paste and rice to oil in pan.

Add one-quarter of liquid to pan; cook and stir until absorbed. Repeat.

When rice is tender, add cooked seafood, clams and lime juice.

Combine garlic, allspice, oregano, cumin, cinnamon, chili, coriander and wine.

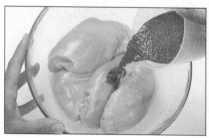

Pour spice mixture over chicken breasts, cover and refrigerate.

CHICKEN

Chicken cooked the Mexican way is, for most of us, a new experience — especially its unusual and surprisingly delicious combination with chocolate.

Spiced Chicken Breasts

Adjust chili to taste.

Preparation time:
10 minutes +
4 hours marinating
Cooking time:
15 minutes
Serves 4

6 cloves garlic	*1 teaspoon ground*
½ teaspoon ground	*cumin*
allspice	*½ teaspoon ground*
1 teaspoon oregano	*coriander*
½ teaspoon ground	*⅓ cup red wine*
cinnamon	*4 chicken breast fillets*
½ teaspoon chili	*2 tablespoons*
powder	*vegetable oil*

1 Place garlic, allspice, oregano, cinnamon, chili powder, cumin, coriander and wine in a food processor. Process 1–2 minutes or until smooth. Set aside.

2 Place chicken in a medium bowl. Pour spice mixture over. Cover and refrigerate for 4 hours.

3 Heat oil in large skillet. Drain marinade from chicken. Cook chicken in batches over medium-high heat 5–7 minutes or until no longer pink, turning once. Serve with fresh vegetables.

Note: Allspice is also called Jamaica pepper because most of the world's allspice comes from Jamaica. It is the dried berry of a tree native to tropical America, and is called allspice because its taste resembles a mixture of several spices.

Drain chicken from marinade; heat oil and cook chicken in batches.

Cook chicken 5–7 minutes or until tender and no longer pink, turning once.

37

Fruity Baked Chicken

Preparation time:
25 minutes
Cooking time:
1½ hours
Serves 4

STUFFING
1 teaspoon lemon juice
1 small onion, chopped
6 ounces mixed dried fruit bits
2 tablespoons butter, melted
½ cup sliced almonds
ground pepper, to taste
½ teaspoon ground cumin

1 3-pound chicken
½ teaspoon ground pepper, extra
½ teaspoon ground cumin, extra
1 tablespoon lemon juice, extra
2 tablespoons butter, melted, extra

---

1 Preheat oven to 350°F. Combine lemon juice, onion, dried fruit, butter, almonds, pepper and cumin in a small mixing bowl. Trim chicken of excess fat. Rinse chicken and pat dry with paper towels. Spoon stuffing into chicken cavity and tie wings and drumsticks securely into place with string. 2 Combine extra pepper, cumin, lemon juice and butter in a small bowl. Brush mixture over chicken. Place on a rack in a roasting pan. Roast for 1¼–1½ hours or until chicken is tender and no longer pink. Allow to stand, covered with foil, 10 minutes. Remove string before serving. Serve with the fruit stuffing and fresh vegetables.

Note: If desired, dried apricots may be substituted for the mixed dried fruit bits.

HINT
Butter a slice of stale bread and place it, butter-side-in, in the opening of the chicken. This will keep the stuffing in place.

Combine all stuffing ingredients in a small bowl and mix well.

Spoon stuffing mixture into chicken cavity and tie wings and drumsticks with string.

Mix together pepper, cumin, lemon juice and melted butter.

Place chicken on a rack in a roasting pan. Brush butter mixture all over the chicken.

Chicken in Roasted Pepper Sauce

Preparation time:
25 minutes
Cooking time:
50–60 minutes
Serves 4

---

2 medium red bell peppers, halved and seeded (see Note)	*1 teaspoon dried oregano*
2 teaspoons olive oil, extra	*1 14½-ounce can diced tomatoes, crushed*
2 pounds chicken pieces	*2 medium yellow or red bell peppers, extra, seeded and sliced*
1 medium onion, finely chopped	
2 cloves garlic, crushed	*chili powder to taste (optional)*
2 green apples, peeled, cored and shredded	

1 Brush red peppers with oil. Broil, skin side up, 3–4 inches from the heat for 10–15 minutes or until skin is black. Cover with damp towel until cool. Peel off skin.

Place roasted peppers in a food processor bowl. Process 30 seconds or until mixture is smooth.
2 Heal oil in skillet. Cook chicken in batches over medium-high heat 5 minutes or until golden brown, turning once. Remove from pan; drain on paper towels.
3 Add onion, garlic, apple and oregano to skillet; cook and stir over low heat. Add tomatoes, red pepper purée and bell pepper slices, stirring for 2 minutes. Return chicken pieces to pan. Bring to boil, reduce heat. Simmer uncovered for 40 minutes or until liquid has reduced and chicken is tender. Season with chilli, to taste. Serve with warmed tortillas.
Note: Grilled red bell peppers have a distinctive smoky flavor.

Grill red pepper halves until skin is black. Cover with damp towel.

Cook chicken pieces in batches for 5 minutes or until golden brown.

Add onion, garlic, apple and oregano to pan and cook over low heat.

Add tomatoes, red pepper purée and bell pepper slices to onion mixture.

Chicken in Chocolate Sauce

Preparation time:
20 minutes
Cooking time:
20 minutes
Serves 4

½ cup all-purpose flour
¼ teaspoon ground cinnamon
1 pound boneless skinless chicken breasts
1 tablespoon olive oil
2 tablespoons butter
1 small onion, finely sliced
1 tablespoon unsweetened cocoa powder
1 tablespoon brown sugar
1 tablespoon tomato paste
⅓ cup red wine
1 cup chicken stock
1 tablespoon sour cream
⅓ cup raisins
sliced almonds, toasted, to garnish

---

1 Preheat oven to 350°F. Combine flour and cinnamon in a medium bowl. Toss chicken breasts lightly in seasoned flour. Shake off excess. Reserve 1 teaspoon of flour mixture. Heat oil and butter in large skillet. Cook chicken over medium-high heat until golden, turning once. Remove from pan; drain on paper towels.

2 Add onion, cocoa powder, sugar and tomato paste to skillet and stir over low heat. Add red wine and stock gradually, stirring over low heat until smooth.

3 Blend sour cream and reserved flour in a small bowl until smooth. Add to onion mixture with raisins; stir over medium heat 2 minutes or until thickened slightly. Remove from heat.

4 Place chicken in an ovenproof baking dish. Pour sauce over chicken. Cover and bake for 15 minutes or until chicken is tender and no longer pink. Sprinkle with toasted sliced almonds.

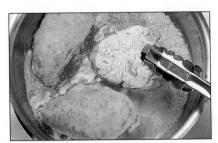

Toss chicken in seasoned flour and then cook in butter and oil until golden.

Stir in onion, cocoa powder, sugar and tomato paste; add wine and chicken stock.

Stir together sour cream and flour until smooth. Add to onion mixture with raisins.

Pour sauce over chicken in dish. Cover and bake until tender and no longer pink.

Heat oil and add onion, tomato paste, chili powder, cumin seeds and tomato juice.

Add stock and crushed tomatoes to pan. Bring to a boil; reduce heat.

VEGETABLES & SALADS

Many Mexican vegetable dishes can be served as a main dish with tortillas or as a course on their own.

Combination Vegetable Stew

Preparation time:
30 minutes
Cooking time:
10–15 minutes
Serves 6

1 tablespoon olive oil
1 small onion, thinly sliced
¼ cup tomato paste
¼ teaspoon chili powder
1 teaspoon cumin seeds
½ cup tomato juice
1 cup vegetable stock

1 14½-ounce can diced tomatoes, crushed
2 small carrots, sliced
2 medium zucchini, halved and sliced
20 green beans
10 ounces cauliflower, cut into small florets

1 Heat oil in large saucepan. Add onion, tomato paste, chili powder, cumin seeds and tomato juice. Stir until well combined.
2 Add stock and crushed tomatoes. Bring to a boil; reduce heat. Add remaining vegetables. Simmer, uncovered, until soft. Serve with fresh tortillas.

Note: Mexicans make this stew with many different vegetable combinations and quite often with leftovers from the previous night. If you use cooked vegetables, they will require only a few minutes in the sauce to heat through. Cook the sauce for 10 minutes before adding the vegetables. Corn, either fresh or dried, is a popular addition to this dish.

Cut vegetables into pieces that will cook at the same time.

Add vegetables to tomato sauce in pan and simmer, uncovered, until soft.

Cheesy Rice-stuffed Peppers

Preparation time:
40 minutes
Cooking time:
30 minutes
Serves 6

---

3 small red bell peppers
3 small green bell peppers
1 tablespoon olive oil
1 small onion, chopped
1/4 teaspoon chili powder
1/2 teaspoon ground cumin
1 teaspoon chicken bouillon granules

3 tablespoons tomato paste
1 cup medium or long grain rice
2 cups water
1 12-ounce can corn kernels, drained
2 jalapeno chili peppers, chopped
1 cup shredded cheddar cheese

---

1 Cut tops off peppers; set tops aside. Carefully remove membranes and seeds from peppers.

2 Heat oil in a medium pan. Stir in onion, chili powder cumin, rice, bouillon granules and tomato paste. Add water. Cover with tight-fitting lid. Bring slowly to a boil; stir once. Reduce heat. Cover and simmer until almost all water is absorbed. Remove from heat. Stand, covered 5 minutes or until all water is absorbed and rice is just tender. Stir in corn, chili peppers and 1/2 cup cheese.

3 Preheat oven to 350°F. Fill each pepper with rice mixture. Sprinkle with remaining cheese. Replace tops. Place peppers on a baking sheet and bake 20–30 minutes or until they have softened slightly. Serve warm accompanied by tortillas and salad. **Note:** Yellow or orange bell peppers can be used in this recipe.

Cut tops off bell peppers and carefully remove membranes and seeds.

Heat oil and add onion, chili powder, cumin, bouillon granules, tomato paste and rice.

When rice is tender, stir in corn, chili peppers and ½ cup shredded cheese.

Fill each pepper with rice mixture; sprinkle with cheese and replace tops.

Hot Chili Corn

A summer starter.

Preparation time:
30 minutes
Cooking time:
10 minutes
Serves 6

3 large ears of corn, sliced into 1-inch rounds	*cilantro*
	1 tablespoon tomato paste
3 tablespoons butter, melted	*¼ teaspoon chili powder, or to taste*
2 tablespoons chopped	*sour cream, to serve*

1 Half fill a large pan with water. Bring to a boil and add corn; reduce heat. Simmer until corn is tender.

Drain.
2 Combine butter, cilantro, tomato paste and chili powder in a large bowl. Add hot

corn. Mix well. Serve immediately with a dollop of sour cream.
Note: If fresh corn is unavailable, use frozen ears of corn. The combination of corn, cilantro and chili powder is a mouth-tingling departure from corn on the cob with butter, salt and pepper. Very popular in Mexico, it may well become your favorite way to eat fresh corn on the cob.

Remove husks from corn on the cob and slice into 1-inch rounds.

Add corn to a pot of boiling water. Simmer until corn is tender. Drain.

Mix together melted butter, cilantro, tomato paste and chili powder.

Add hot corn to the chili mixture and toss well to mix. Serve with sour cream.

48

Sweet and Spicy Lentils

Preparation time:
 10 minutes
Cooking time:
 15–20 minutes
Serves 6

1 cup red lentils	*½ teaspoon ground*
1 small onion, chopped	*cinnamon*
½ teaspoon ground	*¼ teaspoon salt*
cumin	*4 cloves*
⅔ cup water	*1¼ cups orange juice*

1 Wash and drain the lentils and place them in a medium saucepan with the onion, cumin, cinnamon, salt, cloves, orange juice and water. Bring to a boil; reduce heat. Cover and simmer for 15–20 minutes or until liquid is absorbed and lentils are tender, stirring occasionally. Remove cloves and serve warm or at room temperature with your favorite Mexican meat dish. Or, roll up in a tortilla with or without meat to make a burrito.

Note: Brown or green lentils may be used in this recipe instead of red ones. However, they take longer to cook as they are large and break down less easily. Overnight soaking will shorten the cooking time.

Prepare the ingredients: chop onion, juice orange and measure spices.

In a saucepan combine lentils, onion, spices, orange juice and water.

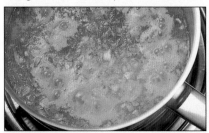

Bring mixture to a boil; reduce heat. Cover and simmer until liquid is absorbed.

The lentils are done when they are very soft. Remove cloves before serving.

Avocado with Lime and Chilies

Preparation time:
20 minutes
Cooking time:
None
Serves 6

---

1 teaspoon finely shredded lime peel	*1 tablespoon chopped fresh parsley*
2 tablespoons lime juice	*2–3 jalapeno chili peppers, seeded and sliced*
1 teaspoon brown sugar	*2 ripe avocados, peeled, pitted and sliced*
1 tablespoon olive oil	

In a small bowl combine lime peel, lime juice, brown sugar, oil, parsley and chili peppers. Whisk until well combined. Spoon over sliced avocados. Serve as a tangy side salad to fish, shellfish, chicken or meat dishes.

Note: The lime dressing will keep for 3–5 days in a covered container in the refrigerator. If limes are unavailable, use lemons instead. You can also cut the avocado into cubes or make into balls with a melon baller (the avocado must be firm), pour over the dressing as above and serve as an appetizer.

Finely shred the lime peel, seed and slice the chili peppers and chop the parsley.

Peel avocado, remove seed and cut into even slices.

Mix together the shredded lime peel, lime juice, sugar, oil, parsley and chili peppers.

Spoon dressing over sliced avocadoes and serve as a side salad.

Tomato Salsa

A Mexican standard.

Preparation time:
10 minutes
Cooking time:
None
Serves 4–6

1 medium tomato, finely chopped	*3 tablespoons lemon juice*
1 medium red onion, finely sliced	*2 teaspoons shredded lemon peel*
2 tablespoons chopped cilantro	

Thoroughly combine all ingredients in a medium bowl. Cover and chill in the refrigerator. Serve as an accompaniment to empanados, tacos, burritos or as a refreshing sauce with meat, chicken or seafood dishes. Or, serve with tortilla chips as an appetizer. **Note:** Use green onions if a milder flavor is preferred. Or add a little finely chopped green or red chili pepper for heat. The size of the tomato and onion will determine the quantity that this recipe makes. It is at its best when eaten fresh, but it can be stored, covered, for up to 2 days in the refrigerator.

Chop the tomato very finely and slice the red onion lengthwise.

Finely chop the cilantro, squeeze lemon juice and shred lemon peel.

Place tomato, onion, cilantro and lemon peel in bowl. Add lemon juice.

Stir well to mix, then cover with plastic wrap and chill in refrigerator.

DESSERTS

Mexicans like their desserts spicy with just a hint of sweetness. Cinnamon and cloves are their favorite dessert spices.

Fresh Fruit with Clove Syrup

Preparation time:
  15 minutes
Cooking time:
  15 minutes
Serves 4–6

½ cup brown sugar
⅓ cup lemon juice
1 tablespoon Triple
  Sec liqueur
¼ teaspoon ground
  cloves

¼ cup water
1 small pineapple,
  cut into thin wedges
2 medium bananas,
  sliced diagonally
2 mangoes, sliced

1 Combine sugar, water, cloves, Triple Sec and lemon juice in a small pan. Stir over low heat until sugar has dissolved. Bring to a boil; reduce heat. Simmer, uncovered, until liquid has reduced by a quarter. Cool.
2 Pour cooled syrup over fruit. Serve.

Combine sugar, lemon juice, water, Triple Sec and cloves in a small pan.

Simmer syrup, uncovered, until liquid has reduced by a quarter of its volume.

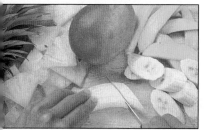

Cut the fruit into attractive and easy-to-eat pieces.

Arrange the fruit in a serving dish and pour over the cooled syrup.

Creamy Chocolate Cinnamon Ring

Preparation time:
  20 minutes +
  overnight standing
Cooking time:
  40–50 minutes
Serves 6–8

¾ *cup sugar*
½ *teaspoon ground cinnamon*
4 *ounces semi-sweet chocolate, chopped*

1¼ *cups heavy cream*
4 *eggs, lightly beaten*
½ *cup milk*

---

1 Preheat oven to 300°F. Brush an 8-inch ring pan or round cake pan with melted butter or oil. Place sugar and cinnamon into a medium heavy-based pan; heat gently without stirring until sugar begins to melt. Stir over low heat until evenly colored and sugar has dissolved. Remove from heat; pour into prepared pan.

2 Combine chocolate and cream in a medium pan. Stir over low heat until chocolate has melted. Remove from heat. Cool slightly.

3 Whisk chocolate mixture, eggs and milk together in a large mixing bowl.

Pour mixture into pan.

4 Stand filled pan in a deep baking dish. Pour in enough warm water to come halfway up the sides. Bake 40–50 minutes or until custard is set and a knife inserted near the center comes out clean. Remove pan from water bath immediately.

5 Cool custard in the pan and refrigerate overnight. Run a flat-bladed knife around the edge of the tin. Invert onto a serving plate. If custard sticks to pan, place a hot, damp cloth over the base of upturned pan for a couple of minutes.

Combine sugar and cinnamon in a pan and heat gently until sugar begins to melt.

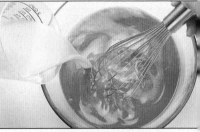

Whisk eggs and milk into cooled chocolate mixture in bowl.

Stand filled pan in baking dish and pour warm water into dish.

Custard is set when a knife inserted near the center comes out clean.

Cinnamon Fritters

Preparation time:
45 minutes
Cooking time:
15 minutes
Makes 36

---

1 cup water
⅓ cup butter
1 cup all-purpose flour
4 eggs, lightly beaten
oil, for deep-frying

CINNAMON SYRUP
½ cup brown sugar
1 cup water
2 tablespoons orange juice
1 teaspoon ground cinnamon

---

1 Combine water and butter in a medium saucepan. Stir over low heat until butter has melted; do not boil.

2 **Remove** pan from heat; add flour all at once. **Beat** until smooth using a wooden spoon. Return to heat. Cook until mixture thickens and comes away from side and base of pan. Remove from heat; cool slightly. Transfer mixture to a small mixer bowl. Add beaten eggs gradually, beating well after each addition until mixture is glossy.

3 Heat oil in a deep pan to 375°F. Gently lower heaping teaspoonsful of mixture into moderately hot oil and cook over medium-high heat 2–3 minutes or until puffed and golden. Remove with slotted spoon. Drain on paper towels. (Split open a fritter to make sure it is cooked in the center.) Serve warm with Cinnamon Syrup.

4 To make Cinnamon Syrup: Combine brown sugar, water, orange juice and cinnamon in a small pan. Stir until sugar has dissolved. Bring to boil. Reduce heat. Simmer until liquid has reduced to three-quarters of its volume Serve warm with Cinnamon Fritters.

Add flour all at once to water and butter and beat until smooth.

Add beaten eggs gradually, beating well after each addition.

60

To make Cinnamon Syrup, combine all ingredients in a small pan.

Remove puffed and golden fritters from oil with a slotted spoon.

Cinnamon Shortbread Cookies

Preparation time:
20 minutes
Cooking time:
10 minutes
Makes 24–28

1½ cups all-purpose flour	1 teaspoon baking powder
½ cup whole blanched almonds, toasted	⅔ cup butter, softened
½ cup light brown sugar	1 egg
⅛ teaspoon salt	2 tablespoons sugar
	¼ teaspoon ground cinnamon

1 Preheat oven to 350°F. Brush a baking sheet with melted butter or oil. Line with parchment paper; grease paper.
2 Place flour, almonds, brown sugar, baking powder, salt, butter and egg in a food processor bowl. Using the pulse action, process for 1 minute until mixture forms a ball.
3 Form level tablespoonsful of dough into balls and flatten. Place on baking sheet.
4 Sprinkle with combined sugar and cinnamon. Bake for 10 minutes. Cool on a wire rack before serving.

Process flour, almonds, brown sugar, butter and egg until it forms a dough.

Take level tablespoons of mixture and roll into balls with your hands.

Flatten balls between the palms of both hands and place on baking sheet.

Mix together sugar and cinnamon and sprinkle over unbaked cookies.

INDEX